PERSPECTIVE

7 STORIES FROM THE BIBLE THAT WILL IMPACT YOUR MINDSET, LIFE, AND LEADERSHIP

By

Dexter J. Peggins Jr.

Table of Contents

Foreword

As church planters, army veterans, and parents of five children, this book assists us in any form of leadership we are called to, helping us understand the importance of maintaining momentum.

Minister Peggins came to the Fall Forward Conference "After Grace" at Restoration Worship Center, Radcliff, Kentucky, and spoke to the leadership. The revelation God gave Minister Peggins from Luke 9:51-56 was so fresh that we are still feasting upon that taught word. He ministered to us about maintaining the high presence of God after the conference and the importance of leadership in our culture today. We must examine where our hearts and spirits are at all times. Transparency gives us accountability to those we serve. Minister Peggins brings transformational teaching that will help you grow as a leader. His teaching changed the lives of the leadership in our church. Therefore, I encouraged him to put this in print for others to be able to read and glean from what we received on that day. This book will be confirmation to some and conviction to others, but most of all, it will be a call to action for anyone who reads it.

Apostle Carl and Donna Smalls
Restoration International Ministries Inc.
Radcliff, Kentucky

Preface

Immediately following a message that I had given to a group of leaders during a church conference, I was approached by one of the participants. With a very intent face, he stated, "Please tell me that you have that message in a book somewhere!" Much to his disappointment, all I could say was, "No, all I have are my notes and outline; everything else is inside me." Before going in a separate direction, with a greater sense of determination, he said, "You have to put your messages in a book." This same individual shared a similar message with me the previous year. On the previous occasion, I thought he was being gracious; however, on this occasion, it was as though I heard him with a different set of ears: I not only heard the demand, I felt it, and I sensed the urgency. I suppose as a means of ensuring that I received the message, the Lord allowed for another individual to walk up to me shortly thereafter and say, "When you write your next book, be sure to put that message in there."

I have had the privilege of teaching biblically-inspired messages and principles for well over a decade, and I have been most fortunate to do so in a number of diverse environments. Whether it has been in a military tent in Iraq, at the bedside of a terminally-ill patient, in churches, in prisons; or even in board room meetings, God has consistently allowed me to be the deliverer of a message that was needed for a particular moment. Similar to those moments in times past, God revealed the need, and He invited me to participate in the solution process.

As I write this book, our world is going through an accelerated period in which we are seeing an increase of apathy, ignorance, and a loss of hope. Domestically, the citizens of the United States have laid witness to an increased number of mass shootings, and there are now reports of innumerable sexual assault cases that have exposed decades-old cultural norms in the arenas of politics, entertainment, and religion. Internationally, we have witnessed the horrors associated with human-trafficking, as revelations of the slave trades in Libya gain national attention. These events, coupled with any number of atrocities that can be found taking place in the world, reveal the global condition of the world we live in. In regard to times such as these, the Prophet Isaiah declares something worth noting:

Arise, shine; for your light has come! And the glory of the Lord is risen upon you. For behold, the darkness shall cover the earth, And deep darkness the people; but the Lord will arise over you, and His glory will be seen upon you. —Isaiah 60:1-2, NKJV

These two verses are loaded with revelation, and I believe they offer insight into how we are supposed to govern ourselves in this day and age. The first thing we should take note of is our posture. This "posture" does not refer to how our bodies are positioned but to how we deal with the issues in our world. We can no longer sit by idly and hope things will change for the better. The command "arise" in this text speaks to coming into right position. Once you are in position, shine or standout in the revelation that God has given you, and be the difference in a world system that is progressively becoming worse.

Hence, I now understand the need to write this book, and to do so at this time. It is incumbent upon all of us who associate ourselves with Jesus Christ that we not only come into understanding of who we are in Him, but also that we realize our authority on this earth. By standing up in the authority that God has given me, the gentlemen who inquired about my teaching at the conference recognized that I was in position to share a revelation that is needed for such a time as this. The request from other people only served to confirm what God was requiring.

The word perspective has several definitions, including "a particular attitude toward or way of regarding something; a point of view." It is with this thought in mind to which this book has been written. The Bible says a great deal about the condition of our minds, and one particular scripture that speaks to the significance of our mental condition can be found in the book of Romans.

And do not be conformed to this world, but be transformed by the renewing of your mind, that you may prove what is that good and acceptable and perfect will of God. —Romans 12:2, NKJV

Our perception greatly influences our ability to successfully engage this world. The wrong perspective of who we are, and more specifically who we are in God, will hinder our ability to live out our God-given purpose. In this book, we will explore several stories from the Bible. The characters in these stories find themselves in some rather unique positions, in which they are confronted with the necessity of addressing their perspective. In these instances, maintaining the status quo would have diverted their ability to move forward into greater levels of increase and personal fulfillment.

I'm not suggesting the lessons presented in this book are the only lessons to be garnered from these particular passages. The Bible is indeed a living book, and as a living book, there is always a new lesson to be gained from the text. What I am endeavoring to present in this book are some simple truths that can be extracted and put into immediate action. This book was written to encourage people dealing with mental barriers that have halted their progress of pursuing purpose. Through these biblical examples, the hope is that the reader will be able to recognize similarities that exist between themselves and the characters being highlighted. Through this process of identification and examination, the reader will come to recognize the availability of solutions to address their own issues.

It is from this place of resolution that we can clearly recognize the significance of our very being. I am a firm believer that your existence is the evidence that the world needs you. You have been born into the generation that needs you the most, and the world is waiting for your contribution; the world is waiting for the light that you carry. If you have yet to accept this truth, I invite you to examine your **Perspective**...

The Reminder of Pain
Moving Forward

This is the genealogy of Terah: Terah begot Abram, Nahor, and Haran. Haran begot Lot. And Haran died before his father Terah in his native land, in Ur of the Chaldeans. Then Abram and Nahor took wives: the name of Abram's wife was Sarai, and the name of Nahor's wife, Milcah, the daughter of Haran the father of Milcah and the father of Iscah. But Sarai was barren; she had no child.

*And Terah took his son Abram and his grandson Lot, the son of Haran, and his daughter-in-law Sarai, his son Abram's wife, and they went out with them from Ur of the Chaldeans to go to the land of Canaan; and they came to Haran and dwelt there. So the days of Terah were two hundred and five years, and **Terah died in Haran**.* —Genesis 11:27-32, NKJV, emphasis added

In my opinion, one of the most thought-provoking stories in the Bible is that of Terah, the father of Abram. Here is a man who after losing a son, decides to relocate his family to another region. While the Bible does not implicitly say what caused Terah to leave the City of Ur, I believe God spoke to Terah and directed him to move to the land of Canaan. While traveling to Canaan, Terah and his family enter into Haran and instead of passing through, they take residency there.

What caused Terah to end his travel prematurely? More specifically, why settle in Haran, a place that shares the same name as his deceased son? In this passage, I believe we see a man whose desire is to start life afresh in a new location; however, the grief of losing a child caused him to settle down in a place that reminded him of his son.

Strong's Concordance defines the name Haran as meaning "mountaineer" (H2039). A mountaineer is recognized as being a native or inhabitant of a mountainous region. In nature, mountains provide safety and places of higher visibility and perspective. Biblically, mountains often represent government and places of prominence. On numerous occasions throughout the Bible, mountains were the location of profound meetings between God and man. Biblically, names were often given in association with the characteristics of the one who has been named. I believe Haran was given his name with the hopes of him becoming a man of oversight and perception. The scriptures do not address if Haran became such a man; however, seeing how he was the father of his brother's wife, and the father of another prominent family member, Lot, I believe his death was of undeniable significance to the family.

Picking up the pieces in pursuit of a new country, Terah leads his family on their pilgrimage to Canaan, and mid-way through the journey, they stop in a mountainous country called Haran, and Terah stays there until his death at the age of 205.

In the story of Terah, we find a man who has been overcome by grief. In a region that provided literal places of oversight (mountains), Terah could not see beyond his hurt. The irony of being in the land of Haran was that the mountains provided the opportunity to view the potential that existed beyond; however, the death of Haran, the son, served as a reminder of unrealized hope and potential.

Does the story of Terah discourage our right to mourn and grieve? Most certainly not! God is Jehovah-Rophe, which literally means "God is healing, restoration, health." God's desire is for us to know Him, and one of His characteristics is that of healing. Healing and restoration would have found Terah in Canaan, the place he originally purposed to go.

This particular story of Terah highlights the danger of allowing emotional hurts to go unchecked. The emotional pain gave way to an environment of depression, and it was in this environment that Terah kept his family, up until his passing. I am certain this environment was harmful, and after Terah's death, God speaks to Abram and tells him to leave his country and his father's house. Abram had to leave his people because they had grown content in a place of unrealized potential, and the only way to recalibrate the destiny of his lineage was for Abram to realign himself with God's instruction. God commands Abram to go to the land of Canaan, and as Abram steps out in obedience, God promises to perpetually bless Abram and make him a great nation (Genesis 12:1-9).

The writer of Psalm 46 declares, "God is our refuge and strength, a very present help in trouble" (Psalm 46:1, NKJV). Pain was never intended to be a place in which we settle. The difficulties we experience in life serve to remind us of our frailties, and most importantly, of our humanity. Within our humanity, the issues that we encounter have the ability to direct us towards a life that is dependent upon God. In this place of dependency, we discover His sufficiency and learn that despite the pain we have endured, there is available strength to help us move forward.

Questions for Consideration

1. Can you recall a time when you were excited about accomplishing a task or goal but stopped short of completing it? What caused you to stop?

2. Are you dealing with any issues or beliefs that have served as barriers to your progress? What are they?

3. Are you in a place, physical or mental, that constantly reminds you of disappointment? What can you do to change the situation?

The Other Side of the Cave
When Destiny Calls

*D*avid therefore departed from there and escaped to the cave of Adullam. So when his brothers and all his father's house heard it, they went down there to him. And everyone who was in distress, everyone who was in debt, and everyone who was discontented gathered to him. So he became captain over them. And there were about four hundred men with him.*

Then David went from there to Mizpah of Moab; and he said to the king of Moab, "'Please let my father and mother come here with you, till I know what God will do for me." So he brought them before the king of Moab, and they dwelt with him all the time that David was in the stronghold.

Now the prophet Gad said to David, "Do not stay in the stronghold; depart, and go to the land of Judah. So David departed and went into the forest of Hereth. —1 Samuel 22:1-5, NKJV

Where do you go when it feels like everyone is against you? Where is your place of rest when it feels like the literal weight of the world is placed squarely on your shoulders? In studying the life of Israel's second king, David, you will discover a life filled with amazing highs and painful lows. With a diversity of life experiences encountered by such a remarkable individual, there are a number of amazing lessons that can be gleaned from his life. One such lesson deals with overcoming obstacles that have been designed to derail us from our destiny.

In 1 Samuel 22, we find David on the run for his life. Several years after killing Goliath and becoming a national hero, David was now being pursued by his father-in-law, King Saul. The obvious question in this situation would be, what did David do to cause such an extreme response by his father-in-law? Did David wrong the king by stealing from him? Did he abuse his wife, the king's daughter? Did he attempt to usurp the king's authority? The answer to these questions is a resounding no. King Saul sought David's life for no other reason than that of jealousy and fear. Due to David's humility and his ever-growing popularity, King Saul began to look upon David as a threat to his throne, and he determined within himself that he would secure his kingdom by killing David. This 22nd chapter picks up shortly after David narrowly escapes one of Saul's numerous attempts to kill him.

Isolated and without a plan, David seeks refuge in the cave of Adullam. While held up in the cave, something very interesting happens: a number of the society's outcast and downtrodden citizens join David in the cave. I imagine these individuals were no different than people we know. These were hard-working people who had high aspirations for their lives. They had hopes and dreams for providing a quality life for their family; however, the trials of life proved too difficult. Life can offer some difficult situations, and enough difficult situations can lead one to feeling overwhelmed and helpless. This was the condition of the people who joined David. They were distressed living in a constant state of anguish, they were in debt, and the lack of relief from their situations caused them to become bitter about the state of their lives. Life had become so difficult that the thought of living in a cave became more appealing than suffering in an unforgiving world. Nevertheless, it would be this cave experience that would undoubtedly be the turning event for their lives. These five verses offer an interesting discourse on how we can handle our own trials when they appear.

Position Yourself to Hear from God

The first takeaway is they positioned themselves to hear from God. Those who merged on the cave were in a place of desperation. Everything about their lives served as a reminder of the direness of their situation, and as a result, they were unable to see any semblance of hope. Bitterness has the potential to rob you of your ability to hear and move forward in the realization of your purpose. Whether intentional or unintentional, what they would soon discover is that by distancing themselves from the distractions and positioning themselves to hear from God, they would soon get instructions that would revolutionize their lives. One of the most critical aspects of what this group of discontented people did was found in their submission to the leadership of David.

As previously mentioned, bitterness has the potential to dull our ability to hear from God; hence, it was critical for this group of people to position themselves in an environment where the leader was able to hear from God. Romans 10:17 declares, "Faith comes by hearing, and hearing by the word of God." In addition to having the heart of a shepherd and being an effective leader, David, was a man attuned to the voice of God. He had already determined within himself that he would not make any decisions until he heard from God; therefore, the people could find solace in knowing that while they were in the cave, they could focus on being restored, and when God spoke, they could trust that the correct response would be given.

The text does not give much detail as to what happened in the cave, nor does it reveal how long they were in the cave; however, a clue as to what transpired can be found in the revelation of the rock. The name Adullam means "justice for man" (Strong's H5725), and I believe that the people who convened inside the cave of Adullam experienced a restorative work. This work addressed the oppression that kept them bound, and it brought mental and emotional healing.

Coming out of the Cave

As those who were in the cave began to receive healing, they gained clarity, and the word of the Lord came shortly thereafter.

Now the prophet Gad said to David, "Do not stay in the stronghold; depart, and go to the land of Judah. So David departed and went into the forest of Hereth. —1Samuel 22:5, NKJV

The instruction that David and those who followed had been waiting on was to leave the cave and go to Judah. The significance of this instruction was not only in the fact that Judah was a different geographical area; the revelation can be found in recognizing that Judah means "praise." What transpired in the cave was a work that was deserving of praise. Praise not only serves as a demonstration of our thankfulness, but it also helps to cultivate an atmosphere of worship, and from this posture, we are able to gain greater access and understanding from God.

What took place in Adullam is akin to what transpires when we seek refuge in Jesus Christ. Jesus Christ is our chief cornerstone. When we surrender to him, we undergo the transformative work of being justified. In this regard, the scriptures declare, "If anyone is in Christ, he is a new creation; old things have passed away; behold, all things have become new" (2 Corinthians 5:17, NKJV). When we go into the cave/rock of Christ, God calls out to the destiny and purpose that exist within the new man. Just as David and those who joined him in the cave went immediately to Judah (praise), we too can rejoice knowing that a transformative work has taken place, and as a result, we release a praise that belongs to God.

Called to Greatness

David could have determined that life was too hard, and he could have decided to stay in the cave; however, he heard the voice of purpose calling out to him, and it compelled him to move forward. David was called to be the king, and his subsequent journey on the other side of the cave would ultimately lead him to assuming that office. In addition to David assuming a place of authority, those who joined him in the cave underwent a transformation in their identities. They were no longer the distressed and discontented; on the contrary, a number of them would go on to be known as David's renowned men, known for accomplishing amazing exploits. What awaits you on the other side of your transformation process? I dare to believe that whatever it is, the world is anxiously awaiting for you to come into the realization of it.

Questions for Consideration

1. **When dealing with stress, what do you do to gain relief?**

2. **When facing adversity and resistance, what is your normal course of action?**

3. **Can you think of any events in your life that have made you bitter or resentful? What did you do to address your feelings?**

Don't Let Your Hang-ups Become Your Hold-ups
Challenging Mindsets

*N*ow it came to pass, when the time had come for Him to be *received up, that He steadfastly set His face to go to Jerusalem, and sent messengers before His face. And as they went, they entered a village of the Samaritans, to prepare for Him. But they did not receive Him, because His face was set for the journey to Jerusalem. And when His disciples James and John saw this, they said, 'Lord, do You want us to command fire to come down from heaven and consume them, just as Elijah did?'*

But He turned and rebuked them, and said, "You do not know what manner of spirit you are of. For the Son of Man did not come to destroy men's lives but to save them." And they went to another village. —Luke 9: 51-56, NKJV

I'm convinced that in many cases, one of the primary reasons we are not seeing victories to greater degrees in our lives is because we have allowed the idols of wrong beliefs to go unchallenged. Limited perspectives are some of the hang-ups that we commonly deal with. If we are not careful, we run the risk of making judgment calls that are contrary to the will of God. The end result is that we miss out on experiencing a harvest that God desires for us to be a part of.

In this story, the disciples James and John find themselves in this very predicament. They made the determination that because this particular region was not receptive to Jesus, the appropriate action would be the destruction of this community. Despite their zeal and self-righteous indignation, they quickly found out they were operating in a manner that was contradictory to the will of God.

At the time of the text, James and John had been with Jesus for a period of at least 3 years. Along with Peter, they were in Jesus' inner circle, and because of their closeness to Jesus, they were privy to experiences that none of the other disciples encountered. One such experience was that of seeing Jesus transfigured on a mountain (Matthew 17). In addition to having a close relationship with Jesus, both John and James had grown into effective ministers, and they were key contributors in several evangelistic campaigns (Mark 6:7-13). Despite being gifted and being in relationship with Jesus, John and James allowed their familiarity with Jesus to put them in a position where they mistakenly assumed their preconceptions and prejudices were the will of God.

There are several points of consideration that I would like to highlight from this passage:

1. James and John failed to consider that, Jesus rarely, if ever, ministered from a place of convenience. When he healed the sick, it was most often done at the behest of the one being

healed. This is worth noting because ministry does not always afford us the opportunity to service others when the conditions are up to our standards. Simply put, we can't always minister to people on our own terms.

Because the Samaritans denied Jesus access, James and John immediately suggested they be destroyed. However, I believe that if they were more sensitive to the situation, they would have realized the Samaritans were operating in a spirit of rejection. The text reveals that because they, the Samaritans, knew Jesus had his mind set on going to Jerusalem and not staying in Samaria, they were upset. For decades, the Samaritans were often ostracized and rejected by the children of Israel. Therefore, when the Samaritans realized Jesus had no intention of staying in Samaria, they were reminded of their years of rejection. The Samaritans wanted an encounter with Jesus, but their hurt caused them to push back.

2. God wants a harvest, and the harvest will come from areas that we deemed helpless. When what James and John believed about the Samaritans was confronted by Jesus, it laid the ground work for another dynamic of their ministry to be realized. Several years after the events of Luke 9, the Bible records the following:

Now when the apostles who were at Jerusalem heard that Samaria had received the word of God, they sent Peter and John to them, who, when they had come down, prayed for them that they might receive the Holy Spirit. For as yet He had fallen upon none of them. They had only been baptized in the name of the Lord Jesus. Then they laid hands on them, and they received the Holy Spirit. —Acts 8:14-17

If John had not resolved the issue in which he was confronted with, he would not have been in a position (emotionally) to usher in this move of God.

The Responsibility of Being

But He turned and rebuked them, and said, "You do not know what manner of spirit you are of. For the Son of Man did not come to destroy men's lives but to save them." —Luke 9:55-56a

At the root of Jesus' rebuke was the fact that James and John lost sight of who they were. Physically, they were in close proximity to Jesus; however, they were far away from Him in their thinking. External situations such as disagreements and rejection should never serve as an occasion for us to get out of character. John and James got out of character, and their belief system concerning the matter was challenged. Ultimately, God knew that in order for John and James to become the type of ministers He was calling them to be, it would be necessary for them to encounter a situation that would reveal the issues of their hearts. The Apostle John, who many refer to as the love apostle, had to be challenged in the area of compassion. This was necessary so he could ultimately grow into the person he was destined to be. Despite the situation and what others around you are doing, the ultimate requirement is to become the person you have been called to be.

Questions for Consideration

1. How receptive are you to embracing thoughts that may challenge your worldview?

2. Can you think of a time when you were required to work with someone you were at odds with? If so, by working together, were you able to get a better understanding of their disposition?

3. Can you think of any worldviews you once believed to be true but now no longer believe?

The Perseverance of Future Generations
The Burden of Responsibility

*A*nd it came to pass, when all the people had completely crossed over the Jordan, that the Lord spoke to Joshua, saying: "Take for yourselves twelve men from the people, one man from every tribe, and command them, saying, 'Take for yourselves twelve stones from here, out of the midst of the Jordan, from the place where the priests' feet stood firm. You shall carry them over with you and leave them in the lodging place where you lodge tonight.'"

Then Joshua called the twelve men whom he had appointed from the children of Israel, one man from every tribe; and Joshua said to them: "Cross over before the ark of the Lord your God into the midst of the Jordan, and each one of you take up a stone on his shoulder, according to the number of the tribes of the children of Israel, that this may be a sign among you when your children ask in time to come, saying, 'What do these stones mean to you?' Then you shall answer them that the waters of the Jordan were cut off before the ark of the covenant of the Lord; when it crossed over the Jordan, the waters of the Jordan were cut off. And these stones shall be for a memorial to the children of Israel forever.'"

And the children of Israel did so, just as Joshua commanded, and took up twelve stones from the midst of the Jordan, as the Lord had spoken to Joshua, according to the number of the tribes of the children of Israel, and carried them over with them to the place where they lodged, and laid them down there. —Joshua 4:1-8, NKJV

In this particular passage, we find the children of Israel at a critical juncture in their journey. They have wandered in the wilderness for 40 years, their leader Moses has just died, and they now find themselves on the cusp of realizing their destiny.

They are at the bank of the Jordan River, and this Jordan serves as the last physical boundary that separates them from the Promise Land they had been hearing about for over 40 years. Now, under the leadership of Joshua, they crossed the Jordan. They were now in the land that had been promised unto them; however, they were yet to receive the promises and benefits associated with their crossing over.

If I could relate this transition into a practical example, I would say this is similar to someone battling alcoholism for years and determining within themselves they will never have another drink. This is similar to an abuse victim determining they will not be tormented again. In these examples, the people have a made the transition in their thinking, but they have yet to know what the mental shift fully entails. I remember having a crossing-over experience a couple of years ago when my wife and I were neck deep in debt. In a moment of frustration and undeniable resolve, we transitioned from the mindset that kept us locked in debt. As evidence of our mounting bills, we were still in debt; however, we determined within ourselves that we would change our behaviors and the subsequent process that we put into place helped our situation to reflect the mental shift we had accepted.

On the Other Side of Frustration

Similar to the children of Israel, before we get to the place of taking away the residue of oppression that has marred us, we must first have a crossing-over moment. Where we pick up in this story, the children of Israel were at their literal and symbolic crossing point; they had not entered into their promise but they were on the other side of the place of their confusion and frustration, which was symbolized by their wandering in the wilderness. It is at this crossing point that God tells them to take 12 large stones (a stone for each tribe) from the midst of the Jordan and carry them to the place where they would be resting. Verse 9 of this chapter reveals something interesting:

Then Joshua set up twelve stones in the midst of the Jordan, in the place where the feet of the priests who bore the ark of the covenant stood; and they are there to this day. —Joshua 4:9)

Joshua set up twelve stones in the midst of the Jordan; however, these were not the same stones that the 12 took from the Jordan. The stones that Joshua set up in the midst of the Jordan were symbolic of the burden the children of Israel had been carrying up to that point. The act performed by Joshua represents the exchange that takes place between God and humanity when we surrender our issues to Him.

Come to Me, all you who labor and are heavy laden, and I will give you rest. Take My yoke upon you and learn from Me, for I am gentle and lowly in heart, and you will find rest for your souls. For My yoke is easy and My burden is light. —Matthew 11:28-30, NKJV

What should not be lost in this realization is the fact that there is still a burden to be carried. When the children of Israel went to the other side with the stones from the Jordan, these stones served as a reminder of the victory that existed in the moment. These stones came from an area (the Jordan) that once served as an obstruction, and as the people carried them to the other side, they became eternal reminders of the victory God had given them.

Does the victory we receive in Christ mean we don't remember the difficulties that existed prior to our breakthrough? Certainly not! Even when the children of Israel were on the verge of their breakthrough, they were still dealing with some of the issues that existed in their lives. You don't wander in the wilderness for 40 years, watching your loved ones die, and not deal with issues of disappointment and shame. There was an emotional reproach that God would eventually remove from them (Joshua chapter 5:9).

Safeguarding Those Behind Us

One of the greatest responsibilities that can be given to anyone is ensuring that those who succeed them are set up for success and are in position to go further than they have. I believe that as it relates to matters such as legacy, this is a burden we should humbly accept. If we are unable to testify of our crossing-over moments, future generations run the risk of experiencing the dangers that exist on the other side of our triumphs.

I previously mentioned that I once experienced the pains of being in debt, and once I made up my mind that I would never be in that position again, my wife and I began to get clarity on how to overcome that issue. We have since gotten the victory in that area, and we are now debt-free. As a father, I have determined there are some battles that my children have no business fighting, especially if I have already gotten victories in those areas. My responsibility now becomes to instruct them on the lessons of victory, while warning them of the dangers that exist when operating outside of wise instruction.

The burden of responsibility mandates that the legacy in which we leave behind is not a people that have to re-fight the battles we have won, but that we prepare those behind us to advance what we have begun.

Here are a few points to consider on this matter:

1. Every legacy has a beginning. Prior to the crossing over of the Jordan, the children of Israel had a legacy. They accepted a legacy that was draped in shame. They experienced God's deliverance from their oppressors in Egypt; however, they were unable to believe in the same God's ability to usher them into their promise, and their 40 years of roaming in the wilderness was a reminder of that.

However, this was not the legacy God intended for them to identify with. God had spoken to this people and declared, "You are to be holy to me because I, the Lord, am holy, and I have set you apart from the nations to be my own" (Leviticus 20:26). Before the children of Israel could experience the fullness of their promise, they had to come into agreement with God's vision for them (Joshua 24:1-28).

2. The carrying of the stones and the erecting of the pillar represented a shift, not only in the mindset of the children of Israel but also as a reminder of what they had overcome. It became a platform of instruction for others. I have the privilege of serving as mentor, minister, and coach. Regardless of the setting or the individual I am speaking with, one of the most common things I encounter is people's inability to let go. There are certain attitudes and beliefs that are hindering people from experiencing the life God wants them to have. What I often share with people is this, "The people behind you are depending upon you to get free from those issues. If you're not free, there is a greater likelihood they will become ensnared by the same detrimental beliefs that held you bound."

Freedom from an issue and masking the pain associated with that issue are not one in the same. Masking the pain implies the issue still has the ability to adversely affect you.

When you have received freedom from an area that once held you bound, you have the ability to acknowledge the issue for what it was and definitively tell someone else how you overcame it.

3. If those who are behind us are close to the rocks, we must also assume they are close to the bondage that exists on the other side. Later books in the Bible reveal that the children of Israel would continue to fall into repetitive cycles of bondage and freedom. There was a continual cycle of forgetting about God, going through adversity, and because the oppression was so great, they would call upon God. Subsequently, they would experience deliverance, and consequently, the cycle would be repeated over again with the next generation.

I'm convinced that one of the greatest disservices we can do unto God is to assume the victories we encounter in life are solely about us. Your breakthrough serves as a key for someone else to be released from their own bondage. There are people in need of the hope, encouragement, and rebuke that come with your breakthrough. This is the responsibility associated with the burden of safeguarding future generations.

Questions for Consideration

1. Can you recall a time you let go of a damaging belief system or habit? What was the circumstance that sparked the change?

2. Are there any detrimental behaviors you are carrying around? What is keeping you from letting them go?

3. What advice would you give someone dealing with detrimental behaviors that are similar to the ones you once dealt with?

The Success Set-up
You Can Do It!

*F*or the kingdom of heaven is like a man traveling to a far country, who called his own servants and delivered his goods to them. And to one he gave five talents, to another two, and to another one, to each according to his own ability; and immediately he went on a journey. Then he who had received the five talents went and traded with them, and made another five talents. And likewise he who had received two gained two more also. But he who had received one went and dug in the ground, and hid his lord's money. After a long time the lord of those servants came and settled accounts with them.*

So he who had received five talents came and brought five other talents, saying, "Lord, you delivered to me five talents; look, I have gained five more talents besides them." His lord said to him, "Well done, good and faithful servant; you were faithful over a few things, I will make you ruler over many things. Enter into the joy of your lord." He also who had received two talents came and said, "Lord, you delivered to me two talents; look, I have gained two more talents besides them." His lord said to him, "Well done, good and faithful servant; you have been faithful over a few things, I will make you ruler over many things. Enter into the joy of your lord."

Then he who had received the one talent came and said, "Lord, I knew you to be a hard man, reaping where you have not sown, and gathering where you have not scattered seed. And I was afraid, and went and hid your talent in the ground. Look, there you have what is yours."

But his lord answered and said to him, "You wicked and lazy servant, you knew that I reap where I have not sown, and gather where I have not scattered seed. So you ought to have deposited my money with the bankers, and at my coming I would have received back my own with interest. Therefore take the talent from him, and give it to him who has ten talents.

"For to everyone who has, more will be given, and he will have abundance; but from him who does not have, even what he has will be taken away." —Matthew 25:14-29, NKJV

One of my all-time favorite speakers was the late Dr. Myles Munroe. Dr. Munroe would often share the following sentiment, "The richest place on earth is the cemetery." Inside the cemetery are inventions, cures, music, books, etc. that people never released into the earth. These gifts went to the grave with the people and as a result, the world missed out.

The truth of this statement hit me particularly hard when I worked as a hospital chaplain. During my tenure as a chaplain, I ministered to close to 3,000 patients. These were patients from all walks of life, dealing with diverse situations. I ministered to parents who lost their children, I was there with patients who had just received terminal diagnoses, I ministered to people who didn't know how they were going to pay their hospital bills on account of losing their job. For as difficult as those conversations were, the hardest conversations I have ever had were with those patients who were at the end of their lives and unable to give an account of what they had done with the life they lived. What consolation can you give to someone filled with regret about living a life of unrealized potential? The saddest detail of these conversations was that each of these patients recognized there was something they were supposed to do, but they allowed the circumstances of life to halt their pursuit.

A Divine Set-up

One of the most important things to know about God is that He is intentional and purposeful. Our very existence is proof that we are alive for a reason. God does not make anything devoid of purpose, and because God is invested in our ability to realize our purpose, He intentionally set us up for success. Here are a few ways in which we have been setup for that success:

1. Everybody Gets Something. The ruler administered the talents based upon the stewards' capacity to produce. Talents weren't given on the pretense of like or dislike; they were given in direct relation to the stewards' ability to work. The gift God has given you is directly connected to your ability to succeed in that area. God is not in the business of setting us up to fail. We are His representation on earth, and we have been called to exercise authority over that in which we have been given. Simply put, if you have a gift, it's because you are able to produce greater from the utilization of it.

2. Success and failure are both predictable. The word ability means the capacity to produce. The Lord has given us the capacity to produce wealth as a sign that we are in an alliance or covenant with Him.

And you shall remember the Lord your God, for it is He who gives you power to get wealth, that He may establish His covenant which He swore to your fathers, as it is this day. —Deuteronomy 8:18, NKJV

Matthew 25:14 says that he (Jesus) gave his goods to his servants. This statement reveals there was a relationship (covenant) that existed between the lord and his servants, and this relationship warranted trust. The lord recognized the servants' abilities, but the servants had to understand they had to put their abilities to work. As the servants went about the task of doing their work, they discovered the harvest associated with the work they performed. Simply put, the two servants who went to work received a harvest, and the one servant who did nothing, received nothing.

3. Your success glorifies God. Our success is not only about the accumulation of wealth and obtaining material possessions; these are benefits. Through the exercising of our gifts and abilities, we are supposed to advance God's kingdom. The kingdom advances when we do the work that has been entrusted to us.

4. There Is an Expectation. The ruler in this passage does not tell the servants what to do with the talents. This implies a deep level of trust that the lord has in his servants' ability to be creative. When the ruler came back, He wanted an account of what the servants did with what they had been given.

Similar to the experiences we encounter in life, I believe the good and faithful servants experienced moments of difficulty and possibly failure as they worked their talents. Nevertheless, nothing is wasted in the kingdom; even failed experiences have great value if we learn from them. I'm sure the good and faithful servants made mistakes, and those mistakes helped them refine their process, and by working out the process, they realized a harvest.

When the wicked servant was called to give an account, he said he knew his Lord was a hard man who reaped where he didn't sow. The wicked servant was fully aware of his Lord's disposition; however, he never considered what it meant for the Lord to give the gift to him. If the Lord was as volatile as the servant believed him to be, wouldn't the servant know that the Lord wouldn't haphazardly give him the talent without first taking into consideration the servant's ability to handle it? If the servant looked at his situation from the right perspective, he would have known that if the Lord could trust him with his goods, then the Lord must have thought very highly of him.

Fear will cause you to take on the wrong perspective about how God feels about you, and as a result, it will cause you to miss out on what God wants you to experience. The simple fact that God gives you a gift should serve as proof that He trusts you with the gift.

The 29th verse of this chapter reveals an undeniable truth.

For to everyone who has, more will be given, and he will have abundance; but from him who does not have, even what he has will be taken away.

Everyone has something, but when you are unable to see what you do have, you will disregard it. Once you disregard your gift, you will ultimately lose it because it holds no value to you. God is invested in our success, and He has equipped you with everything you need to live a life of purpose. Don't discredit the gifts that will help you succeed in life!

Questions for Consideration

1. What gifts and talents do you have at your disposal? How are you utilizing your gifts?

2. Name a few ways you can become more effective in your areas of gifting.

3. At the end of your life, how would you like to be remembered? What are you doing now to ensure this will be the case?

You're a Decision Away
Choosing Destiny

A nd when Jesus saw great multitudes about Him, He gave a command to depart to the other side. Then a certain scribe came and said to Him, "Teacher, I will follow You wherever You go."

And Jesus said to him, "Foxes have holes and birds of the air have nests, but the Son of Man has nowhere to lay His head."

Then another of His disciples said to Him, "Lord, let me first go and bury my father."

But Jesus said to him, "Follow Me, and let the dead bury their own dead." —Matthew 8:16-22, NKJV

Have you ever wondered how social movements begin? What was the catalyst that prompted Martin Luther to challenge the Catholic Church in the year 1517, at the height of the Catholic Church's social authority? In nailing his 95 Theses to door of the Wittenberg Castle church, Luther challenged a number of the unpopular practices that church instituted. This act ultimately led a series of events that paved the way for the development of the Protestant movement. What was the catalyst that led Martin Luther King Jr. to champion the cause of civil rights during a racially averse time of U.S. history? By all accounts, Dr. King could have settled into his role as pastor and subsequently let the civil rights movement progress without his involvement. Nevertheless, he acknowledged his beckoning call and became one of the prominent voices during this time. I am convinced movements begin and continue when people dare to believe and make a decision to act.

In this passage of scripture, we find Jesus Christ extending an invitation of companionship to one of His disciples. Strong's defines the term disciple as being a pupil (G3129); hence, this man was a student of Jesus. As a disciple, this man would have committed himself to the personal discipline of adhering to the teachings of Jesus Christ. As a disciple, he had postured himself to wait on the call from the Lord; nevertheless, similar to the cases of both Martin Luther and Martin Luther King Jr., the invitation to enter into the movement that God has for you may come at a point in life when it seems to be most inconvenient.

Ideal Timing vs. God's Perfect Timing

In this passage of scripture, the disciple verbalized his desire to follow Jesus; however, he acknowledged the need to bury his father. For all intents and purposes, this was noble deed and an honorable service unto his father. Nevertheless, despite how well intentioned his request, his response revealed the condition of his heart. He said, "Lord, let me first," which is indicative of order of priority and importance.

Similar to the disciple in the scripture, many of us find ourselves in this place of tension with God. The disciple's statement is symbolic of telling God, "Wait for me until I get my stuff together," "God, I'm with you, but let me do this first," or "Let me stop doing this and I will follow you." I am convinced that as it relates to God, our difficulty will not always be in believing in God's ability; often, are struggles are wrapped up in thinking the conditions of our participation must first be perfect.

Destiny rarely happens in the conformity of our perfectly laid-out plans. We must accept that perfect timing and ideal timing are not one in the same. Perfect timing, within the context of God's will is when God invites you to participate in a move in which He will be glorified. Ideal timing is when the perceived conditions are favorable for you to move. Ideal timing speaks to convenience; God's perfect timing speaks to shifts that change oppressive mindsets and systems.

The 11th chapter of John highlights several examples of the ideal and perfect timing dynamic.

1. God's perfect timing:

Then Jesus said to them plainly, "Lazarus is dead. And I am glad for your sakes that I was not there, that you may believe. Nevertheless let us go to him." —John 11:14-15, NKJV

Jesus said, "Take away the stone." Martha, the sister of him who was dead, said to Him, "Lord, by this time there is a stench, for he has been dead four days." Jesus said to her, "Did I not say to you that if you would believe you would see the glory of God?" —John 11: 39-40, NKJV

2. Ideal timing:

Now Martha said to Jesus, "Lord, if You had been here, my brother would not have died." —John 11:21, NKJV

Then, when Mary came where Jesus was, and saw Him, she fell down at His feet, saying to Him, "Lord, if You had been here, my brother would not have died." Therefore, when Jesus saw her weeping, and the Jews who came with her weeping, He groaned in the spirit and was troubled. And He said, "Where have you laid him?" They said to Him, "Lord, come and see." Jesus wept. Then the Jews said, "See how He loved him!" And some of them said, "Could not this Man, who opened the eyes of the blind, also have kept this man from dying?" —John 11: 32-37, NKJV

Within the context of ideal timing, our decision to act is often based upon our ability to hide our vulnerabilities. Often, if the situation does not allow for us to be seen in the best light or showcase our strengths, we have a tendency to shrink back. Nevertheless, God's grace is sufficient and His strength is made perfect in our weakness (2 Corinthians 12:9); hence, the significance of God's perfect timing is predicated upon God being glorified in an action that could have not been accomplished without His involvement.

The Need to Act

Our decisions to respond to the timing of God have direct implications on the fulfillment of our purpose. Consider the man who wanted to bury his father. Jesus extended an invitation for this man to partner in his work. Shortly after their encounter with one another, Jesus would find himself bringing deliverance to a man who lived amongst the tombs because he was vexed with demonic spirits (Matthew 8:28-34). Jesus was inviting the disciple, whose focus was on his dead father, to minister a word of life to a man living among the dead.

When God invites us to a work, we never know the full magnitude of what God is calling us too. This same demon possessed man who was delivered went on to spread the news of what Jesus had done for him (Mark 5:18-20). The 7th and 8th chapters of Mark highlight how Jesus went on to do miracles in the town of this man. One such miracle was the feeding of the 4000. Within the scope of the disciple who wanted to bury his father, unbeknownst to him, he had the opportunity to be a part of this work.

Nevertheless, as it relates to the disciple who wanted to bury his father, something very interesting must be noted.

But Jesus said to him, "Follow Me, and let the dead bury their own dead." Now when He (Jesus) got into a boat, His disciples followed Him. —Matthew 8:22-23, NKJV

The text does not expressly say if the man who wanted to bury his father did or did not get on the boat. The text says the disciples followed Jesus, which suggests that the man may have joined Jesus on his journey.

A fundamental key as it relates to making a decision for what ignites and sustains a God-move is this: **You have to SEE the joy BEYOND the sacrifice (Hebrews 12:2)**. The reward on the other side of your decision has to be bigger to you, than what you are being asked to let go.

Questions for Consideration

1. **Can you recall a time when you hesitated on taking advantage of a unique opportunity? What caused the hesitation?**

2. **If a once-in-a-lifetime opportunity became available to you today, would you be able to take it? What factors would be at play concerning your ability to make a decision?**

For Such a Time as This
You are the Change Agent

or if you remain completely silent at this time, relief and deliverance will arise for the Jews from another place, but you and your father's house will perish. Yet who knows whether you have come to the kingdom for such a time as this? —Esther 4:14, NKJV

I have the privilege of wearing a number of diverse hats. Some people know me as a reverend, some people know me as a life coach, others know me as a motivational speaker. Regardless of the audience, a recurring message I often share is, "Your birth is evidence that the world needs you." Upon making this declaration, I am often greeted with some unique responses. I hear things like, "I'm just a single parent, trying to get ahead of my bills. What can I offer the world?" I also get responses like, "Certainly you're mistaken, because I'm not good at anything, let alone helping the world." Despite the objections, one thing that must be agreed upon is the fact that God was very intentional in our creation. Scientists believe that anywhere between 40 million and 1 billion sperm are released during the conception process. If any other sperm would have fertilized the egg, we would not have been conceived. In the Psalm 139, David records the following:

For You formed my inward parts; You covered me in my mother's womb. I will praise You, for I am fearfully and wonderfully made; Marvelous are Your works, And that my soul knows very well. — Psalm 139: 13-14, NKJV

Our inability to see ourselves as greater is often rooted in a limited mindset that was shaped by any number of negative circumstances that occurred over a course of time. Despite our grit and resolve, the adversities, traumas, disappointments, etc. that we often face have the tendency to take wind from our sails. Without any reprieve, we can find ourselves surrendering the life we desire to live, and as a consequence, we find ourselves existing but not truly living. It is from this place of tension that I believe the story of Esther takes on a greater sense of relevance.

Esther was a slave girl living in Babylon during the time of Jewish captivity. In addition to being a slave, Esther was also an orphan who was raised by her cousin Mordecai. As a young woman, Esther experienced objectification on the basis of her looks. A royal decree went out across the land stating that all of the beautiful girls within the region must be separated and placed in the king's harem, and on account of Esther's beauty, she was sent to the king's citadel. If this wasn't enough, prior to becoming a part of the king's harem, Esther was told by her surrogate father (Mordecai) that she had to keep the identity of her people and her family a secret.

Responding to the Call

And Mordecai told them to answer Esther: "Do not think in your heart that you will escape in the king's palace any more than all the other Jews. For if you remain completely silent at this time, relief and deliverance will arise for the Jews from another place, but you and your father's house will perish." —Esther 4:13-14a, NKJV

In observing the situations surrounding the life of Esther, one may notice themes of rejection, abandonment, isolation, and as previously mentioned, objectification. Subconsciously, these themes served as significant mental barriers that remained with Esther until the circumstances of her life demanded they be dealt with. Esther would obtain favor while she resided in the harem, and eventually she became queen; however, even with the title of queen, it would not be until she addressed her vulnerabilities that she would truly master her position of authority.

A man by the name of Haman was the king's right-hand man. He ascended to a place of authority, and with his ascension, servants would pay respect to him by bowing. Mordecai, Esther's paternal figure, enraged Haman on account of his unwillingness to bow to him. In essence, the servants were worshipping Haman, and as a Jew, Mordecai's worship was intended for God and God only. Because Mordecai was unwilling to bow, Haman felt slighted and he devised a plan to have all of the Jews within the region killed. Haman lied to the king and stated that there was a group of people in the region that didn't obey the king's law and as a result it was necessary to eliminate this group. Unbeknownst to the king, this group Haman referred to was the Jews, the same community in which his new queen was a member of.

It is at this intersection of life and death that Mordecai presents the most revealing question that Esther would ever encounter: "How do you know that you have not been called for such a time as this?" Understandably, she was nervous. Esther understood the severity of the situation and she was fully aware of the implications that existed with any hasty action. Death was the result of anyone attempting to see the king unannounced, and even though she was the queen, she too needed authorization. Nevertheless, Esther undoubtedly came to recognize that the circumstances of her life were not coincidental. The events of her life prepared her for this moment, and she would answer the call to act.

Then Esther told them to reply to Mordecai: "Go, gather all the Jews who are present in Shushan, and fast for me; neither eat nor drink for three days, night or day. My maids and I will fast likewise. And so I will go to the king, which is against the law; and if I perish, I perish!" —Esther 4:15-16, NKJV

The greatest responsibility you have in life is to become the person God has called you to be. Adversity served as the catalyst to launch Esther into her purpose. After the 3-day fast, Esther approached the king and found favor in his sight. She would devise her own plan that would ultimately lead to the preservation of her people and the death of Haman.

God often uses adversity as the springboard for us to discover and engage our purpose. Quite often, the nature of the issue that must be addressed will often be presented in a way in which we innately know we must respond. Similar to Esther, we will recognize that the events of our lives have prepared us for the given moment. Never devalue the experiences of your life; they may be used as the platform in which you will be able to help others.

Questions for Consideration

1. **Have you identified your purpose in life? Can you identify your "for such a time as this" moment? If so, what was it?**

2. **What events in life have helped to prepare you for where you are now? When going through the events, did you see their value in the moment?**

3. **How do others benefit from your experiences?**

About The Author

Dexter Peggins Jr., is the CEO and Founder of Kingdom Solutions Consulting. With a practical approach to advisement and a desire to help people reach the fullness of their potential, Dexter is quickly becoming a sought out leader in the area of life transformation. For close to 20 years, Dexter has helped countless people experience transformation in their personal, professional, and spiritual lives. Dexter's mantra is simple; "Live a Life of Purpose, on Purpose!"

Having an innate ability to inspire, motivate, and instruct; Dexter serves as a mentor, adviser, and consultant to business and spiritual leaders going through transition, and emerging leaders looking to make their mark in the world.

Dexter is a husband, father, business owner, author, veteran, a leader, political influencer, and most importantly an Ambassador of God. He holds a Bachelor's degree in Christian Ministry, and a Master of Public Administration. In addition to being a business owner, he serves on the boards of the New Leaders Council, The Re-Entry Initiative, Department of Juvenile Justice, and My Brother's Keeper (Augusta, GA).

For more information, visit: www.dexterpegginsjr.com

www.ingramcontent.com/pod-product-compliance
Lightning Source LLC
Chambersburg PA
CBHW030304030426
42337CB00012B/578